HOUGHTON MIFFLIN
Reading

Talent
Show

HOUGHTON MIFFLIN   BOSTON

Printed in the U.S.A.

ISBN 0-618-33724-2

4 5 6 7 8 9 10-BS-12 11 10 09 08 07 06 05

Design, Art Management, and Page Production: Silver Editions.

Contents

Our Classroom Zoo Book

by Linda Dunlap
illustrated by Mick Reid

Miss Moon's class made a zoo book.
It took us hours in the art room.

1

Miss Moon has cool art tools! We drew with pencils and markers. We found paints in every color, or hue. We shared the paints to be fair. We also used glue and paper. We even made our own paste!

I drew a moose with droopy eyes.
That moose looked sad! I just knew I
would paint him blue.

3

Lou made a cool trout. She drew that
trout with sparkling glue! Then she
painted it gold inside the glue lines. She
might paint a bunch of those trout!

4

Mansoor drew a very good goose. He saw a goose land on the ground. The goose stood very still. Mansoor looked at that goose while he drew. But then that goose flew away.

Sue drew zoo workers. One woman
was cleaning with a broom. Another
zoo helper was cooking food. It looked
like they were having a good time.

6

Miss Moon keeps our zoo book in our room. We add new art too. That zoo book makes us proud.

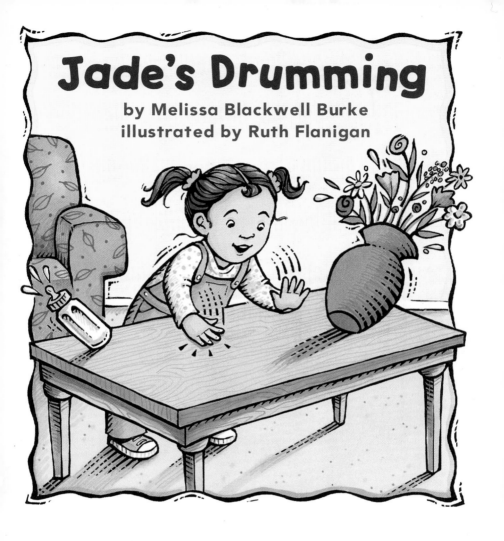

Jade's Drumming

by Melissa Blackwell Burke
illustrated by Ruth Flanigan

Tap! Tap! Tap! Tap! Tap! Tap!
When Jade was a baby, she began
drumming. She rapped and tapped
and patted on everything.

9

When Jade grew up some, she still
drummed. She drummed when she was
planning her day. She drummed when
she was shopping. She drummed when
she was sitting in the tub. Jade was
forever drumming.

"You're bugging me with so much drumming," her sister would say.

But Jade never stopped. She just kept right on drumming.

"I like the sound," Jade would say. "Don't you like it too?"

At times her mother would say, "Jade, the baby is napping. Would you please stop drumming?"

Jade would say, "Yes, Mom, I will stop." Then she would drum outside.

12

When Jade and her sister rode the
bus, Jade would do her drumming. It
didn't matter if Jade's sister grabbed her
drumsticks. Jade would just start patting
her lap or tapping on the window.

"You're bugging me with so much
drumming," her sister would say.

"I'm sorry," Jade would say. "I just
like the sound so much."

When Jade grew up, she did become a very good drummer. She asked her sister to go to a show. Her sister nodded, and off they went.

At the show, Jade did her drumming. Her sister did not say that Jade was bugging her with so much drumming. Instead, she clapped and bragged, "That's my sister drumming!"

Jade waved to the crowd. The crowd
stood up and clapped and clapped.

Jade's drumming made a lot of people
very happy!

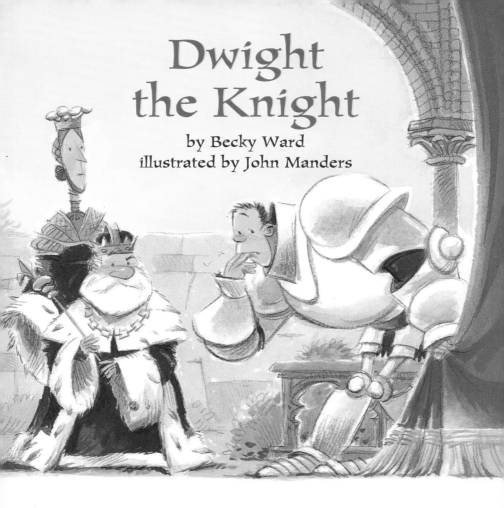

Dwight
the Knight

by Becky Ward
illustrated by John Manders

Sir Dwight had many talents. Queen
Fair and King Mighty felt that Sir
Dwight served them very well indeed.
There was just one problem. Sir Dwight
would not fight.

"My heart is not in it. This knight just can't fight," said Sir Dwight.

"But knights must fight," insisted King Mighty. "That is what knights do."

"Well, that is not what this knight does," said Sir Dwight. "Must I serve you in battle? I am able to serve you in so many other ways."

18

"I can fix you a feast and do it up right. I'll stir up a fine beef stew and then bake you my best lemon pie," said Sir Dwight brightly.

"Sir Dwight, you are a fine cook," said Queen Fair. "But knights must go out and fight."

"I can tell you my best stories each night at bedtime. My mind is filled with wonderful tales. Some will delight you and others will fill you with fright," said Sir Dwight.

"Sir Dwight, we really like the way you tell tales," said King Mighty. "But knights must go out and fight."

"I can paint you pictures of beautiful sights," said Sir Dwight.

"And your paintings are delightful," said the queen. "But really, Sir Dwight, knights must go out and fight."

21

"I can say the alphabet while I dance
a jig. I can run like lightning each time
you call. I can stitch you silk sheets that
make sweet dreams each night," said Sir
Dwight.

The knight went down on his knees.
"I will try to grow wings and then take
flight. But please, please, PLEASE don't
make me fight," cried Sir Dwight.

22

Then King Mighty spoke, "All right, Sir Dwight. It is not right to make you fight if you can't. Tell me, can you be a stay-at-home knight and serve us with your fine talents?"

Sir Dwight hugged King Mighty. "Yes, yes, yes! Yes I can!" he cried.

And that's what he did for the rest of his life!

Who Drew the Cartoon?

by Becky Ward
illustrated by Len Epstein

When you look at a cartoon strip,
do you ever wonder who drew it?
An artist with lots of talent spent a
long time drawing that cartoon!

First, an artist has to think up a funny
story to tell. Then he plans what will go
in each drawing.

26

Next the artist sketches the main
things that go in each box of the cartoon
strip. He uses pencil in case he goofs!
He draws balloons and writes words
in them, too.

Then the artist draws in the
background. Some cartoon drawings
need lines to show the walls in a room.
Others need the moon or a few trees
and clouds.

After that, the artist traces his pencil
lines with ink. He uses fine pens,
brushes, and art tools for adding lines
and dots that look like shadows. An
artist can cut out and glue patterns on
the cartoon, too.

29

Last, the artist chooses colors for the cartoon. He picks bright shades of blue, green, red, and yellow. Then he sends the comic strip to be printed.

So you see, it is true. It takes time and talent to draw a cartoon. Can you think up an idea for a funny cartoon? Maybe you will invent a new comic strip!

Will Holly Sing?

by Anne Walker
illustrated by Anne Kennedy

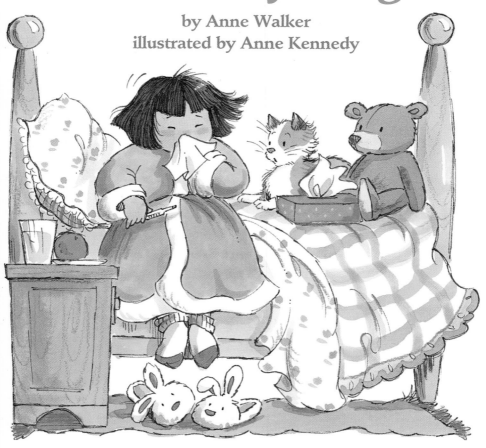

Holly sat up in bed.

"My cold is horrible," whined Holly.

Then she sneezed.

"I hope I can sing at the show."

Holly went to see her neighbor, Luke.

"My head is so stopped up, Luke," she
wheezed. "How will I hear the band?"

Luke gave her warm soup and some
advice.

"Spend the day outside. The fresh air
should help your head," he explained.

Holly laced up her skates. She went skating in town, while her mom went shopping.

She glided past the drug store. She raced past Elmer's Hardware.

Soon she was smiling. But her head was still stopped up.

"Greetings, Holly," said Tom, the owner of Tom's Toys. He was placing three toy bears below a bench outside his shop.

"Good day," Holly replied, waving.

"Look out!" Tom shouted, but it was too late.

Crash! Holly wiped out just past Tom's store.

Tom raced to help Holly up.

She felt a little dazed. She stroked her scraped leg.

Then she shook her head.

"Are you all right?" Tom asked.

"I'm super!" Holly replied. "My head feels better."

"So falling down fixed things up!" joked Tom.

Tom helped her inside his shop. He gave her some freshly baked apple pie.

That night Holly sang in the show.
Smiling, she said, "My first number is
for Tom and Luke."

Then she sang "Good Friends."

Fright Night

by Anne Walker
illustrated by Sarah Brittain

Miss Knight's class was getting set for Fright Night. They hung a banner outside the school.

"Fright Night will be the best night this year," cried Betsy. "I can't wait."

Many people came to see the show
for Fright Night. Mothers and fathers
found seats. Bright lights shone on the
stage. Miss Knight said, "Steve Gilbert
will go first."

Steve sat in the spotlight on Miss Knight's stool. He wore a green tie. He told a tale. In this tale a creature named Mighty Max lived in the woods. A brave boy made friends with this creature, and found out he was as gentle as a lamb.

Next, it was Sally's turn. Sally told
about the high flight of six bats. She
showed pictures of real bats. Then she
yelled "BOO!" and ran off the stage.

44

Kenny dressed up for his spider
dance. He was quite a sight. He wore a
black cape cut in strips. The strips hung
like a spider's legs. Kenny finished his
dance and bowed.

Sue and Shelly wore matching dresses with bright red tights. They tossed three glowing tubes back and forth like jugglers. Then Sue sang a spooky tune while Shelly played the sax.

46

The show ended with a tune sung by
the whole class. The parents stood up
and clapped. Everyone asked to have
Fright Night again next year.

"We just might do that," sighed Miss
Knight.

Word List

Our Classroom Zoo Book (p. 1) accompanies *The Art Lesson.*

DECODABLE WORDS

Target Skill
Vowel Pairs *ew, oo, ou, ue*
blue, book, broom, classroom, cooking, cool, drew, droopy, flew, food, found, glue, good, goose, ground, hue, knew, looked, Lou, Mansoor, Moon, Moon's, moose, new, proud, room, stood, Sue, too, took, tools, trout, zoo

Words Using Previously Taught Skills
add, and, away, art, at, be, bunch, but, class, cleaning, has, having, he, helper, him, in, inside, it, just, keeps, land, like, lines, made, makes, markers, might, Miss, on, or, paints, paint, painted, paste, pencils, sad, saw, shared, she, sparkling, still, that, then, those, time, us, used, very, we, while, with

HIGH-FREQUENCY WORDS

New
fair, gold, woman

Previously Taught
a, also, another, color, even, every, eyes, flour, hours, I, of, one, our, own, paper, school, the, they, to, was, were, workers, would

Jade's Drumming (p. 9) accompanies *The Art Lesson.*

Target Skill (Review)

Structural Analysis: Base Words and Endings -*ed*, -*ing*

bragged, bugging, clapped, drummed, drumming, grabbed, napping, nodded, patted, patting, planning, rapped, shopping, sitting, stopped, tapped, tapping

Words Using Previously Taught Skills

and, asked, at, bus, but, crowd, day, did, didn't, drum, drummer, drumsticks, forever, go, good, grew, happy, her, if, in, is, it, Jade, Jade's, just, kept, lap, like, lot, made, matter, me, mom, mother, much, my, never, not, on, or, outside, please, right, rode, say, she, show, sister, so, sorry, sound, start, still, stood, stop, tap, that, that's, then, times, too, tub, up, very, waved, went, when, will, with, window, yes, you

Previously Taught

a, baby, become, began, do, don't, everything, I, I'm, instead, of, off, people, some, the, they, to, was, would, you're

Dwight the Knight (p. 17) accompanies *Moses Goes to a Concert.*

Target Skill

Long *i* *(igh, ie)*
brightly, cried, delight, delightful, Dwight, fight, flight, fright, knight, knights, lightning, mighty, night, pie, right, sights

Words Using Previously Taught Skills

able, am, and, at, bake, battle, be, bedtime, beef, best, but, can, can't, cook, dance, did, don't, down, dreams, each, feast, felt, fill, filled, fine, fix, for, go, grow, had, he, his, home, hugged, if, in, indeed, insisted, is, it, jig, just, king, knees, lemon, life, like, make, me, must, my, not, on, out, paint, paintings, pictures, please, problem, queen, really, rest, run, say, serve, served, sheets, silk, sir, so, spoke, stay, stew, stir, stitch, sweet, take, talents, tales, tell, that, that's, them, then, this, time, try, up, us, very, way, ways, we, well, went, while, will, wings, with, wonderful, yes, you

New
alphabet, heart, mind

Previously Taught
a, all, are, beautiful, call, do, does, fair, head, I, I'll, many, of, one, other, others, said, some, stories, the, there, to, was, what, would, your

Who Drew the Cartoon? (p. 25) accompanies *Moses Goes to a Concert.*

Target Skill (Review)
Vowel Pairs *ew, oo, ou, ue*
balloons, blue, cartoon, chooses, drew, few, glue, goofs, moon, new, room, too, tools, true, you

Words Using Previously Taught Skills
adding, after, an, and, art, artist, at, background, be, box, bright, brushes, can, case, clouds, comic, cut, dots, draw, drawing, drawings, draws, each, ever, fine, first, for, funny, go, green, has, he, his, in, ink, invent, is, it, last, like, lines, look, lots, main, maybe, need, next, on, or, out, patterns, pencil, pens, picks, plans, printed, red, see, sends, shades, shadows, show, sketches, so, spent, strip, takes, talent, that, tell, them, then, things, think, time, traces, trees, up, uses, when, will, with, wonder, writes, yellow

Previously Taught
a, colors, do, idea, long, of, others, some, story, the, to, walls, what, who, words

DECODABLE WORDS

Target Skill

Base Words and Endings *-ed, -ing*

baked, dazed, glided, joked, laced, placing, raced, scraped, skating, smiling, sneezed, stroked, waving, wheezed, whined, wiped

Words Using Previously Taught Skills

advice, and, apple, asked, at, band, bed, bench, better, but, can, crash, day, down, drug, Elmer's, explained, feels, felt, first, fixed, for, fresh, freshly, gave, good, greetings, hardware, he, help, helped, her, his, Holly, hope, horrible, how, in, inside, is, it, just, late, leg, little, look, Luke, mom, my, night, number, out, outside, owner, past, pie, replied, right, sang, sat, see, she, shook, shop, shopping, shouted, show, sing, skates, so, soon, soup, spend, still, stopped, store, super, that, then, things, three, Tom, Tom's, too, town, toy, toys, up, went, while, will, you

HIGH-FREQUENCY WORDS

New

below, neighbor, should

Previously Taught

a, air, all, are, bears, cold, falling, friends, head, hear, I, I'm, of, said, some, the, to, warm, was, your

Fright Night (p. 41) accompanies *The School Mural.*

Target Skill (Review)

Long *i* as *igh, ie*

bright, cried, flight, fright, high, Knight, Knight's, lights, might, mighty, night, sighed, sight, spotlight, tie, tights

Previously Taught

about, and, as, asked, back, banner, bats, be, best, Betsy, black, boo, bowed, boy, brave, by, came, can't, cape, clapped, class, creature, cut, dance, dressed, dresses, ended, fathers, finished, first, for, forth, found, gentle, getting, Gilbert, glowing, go, green, he, his, hung, in, it, jugglers, just, Kenny, lamb, legs, like, made, matching, Max, Miss, mothers, named, next, on, out, outside, parents, pictures, played, quite, ran, real, red, Sally, Sally's, sang, sat, sax, seats, see, set, she, Shelly, shone, show, showed, six, spider, spider's, spooky, stage, Steve, stood, stool, strips, Sue, sung, tale, that, then, this, three, tossed, tubes, tune, turn, up, wait, we, while, whole, will, with, woods, wore, yelled

HIGH-FREQUENCY WORDS

Previously Taught

a, again, do, everyone, friends, have, I, lived, many, of, off, people, said, school, the, they, to, told, was, year

HIGH-FREQUENCY WORDS TAUGHT TO DATE:

Grade 1	carry	friend	long	pull	today	believe	move
a	caught	full	look	put	together	below	neighbor
able	children	funny	love	read	too	between	order
about	cling	garden	many	ready	try	board	pair
above	cold	girl	me	right	turn	bought	poor
afraid	color	give	minute	room	two	brother	quiet
after	come	go	more	said	under	brought	reason
again	could	goes	morning	saw	upon	busy	roll
against	cow	gone	most	school	very	care	should
all	dance	good	mother	second	walk	child	soldier
already	divide	green	my	see	wall	clothes	special
also	do	grow	near	seven	want	different	stand
always	does	happy	never	shall	warm	during	story
and	done	hard	not	sharp	was	early	straight
animal	door	have	now	she	wash	even	surprise
any	down	he	ocean	shoe(s)	watched	fair	told
are	draw	head	of	shout	water	field	touch
arms	eat	hear	off	show	we	floor	trouble
around	edge	her	old	sing	wear	front	uncle
away	eight	here	on	small	were	gold	until
baby	else	hold	once	so	what	great	war
bear	enough	horse	one	some	where	guess	weigh
because	evening	house	only	soon	who	hair	whole
been	ever	how	open	start	why	half	winter
before	every	hungry	or	sure	work	heard	woman
began	fall	hurt	other	table	world	heart	word
begin	family	I	our	talk	would	heavy	year
bird	far	idea	out	tall	write	hour	young
blue	father	in	over	teacher	you	important	
body	find	is	own	the	your	instead	
both	first	jump	paper	their		kitchen	
break	five	kind	part	there	**Grade 2**	lady	
brown	flower	know	people	these	across	later	
build	fly	laugh	person	they	ago	letter	
butter	follow	learn	picture	thought	air	lion	
buy	for	light	piece	three	alphabet	listen	
by	forest	like	play	through	aunt	middle	
call	found	little	present	tiny	beautiful	million	
car	four	live	pretty	to	behind	mind	

Decoding Skills Taught to Date: Short Vowels *a, i;* Base Words and Endings *–s, -ed, -ing;* Short Vowels *o, u, e;* VCCV Pattern; Long Vowels *a, i* (CVC*e*); Long Vowels *o, u, e* (CVC*e*); Two Sounds for *g;* Consonant Clusters *r, l, s;* Two Sounds for *c;* Double Consonants; VCV Pattern; Final *k* and *ck;* Consonant Digraphs *th, wh, sh, ch,* (*tch*); Base Words and Endings *–er, -est;* Vowel Pairs *ai, ay;* Compound Words; Vowel Pairs *ow, ou;* Suffixes *–ly, -ful;* Vowel Pairs *ee, ea;* Common Syllables *–tion, –ture;* r-Controlled Vowels *ar, or, ore;* Words with *nd, nt, mp, ng, nk;* Base Words and Endings *-s, -es, -ies;* Vowel Pairs *oa, ow;* Final Syllables and Endings; *r*–controlled vowels; The *–er* Ending in Two-Syllable Words; Contractions; The *–le* Ending in Two-Syllable Words; Sound of *y* at the End of Longer Words; Prefix *un–;* Base Words and Endings *–ed, –ing* (Double Final Consonant); Silent Consonants *gh, kn, b;* Homophones; Decoding Multisyllable Words; Vowel Pairs *oo, ew, ue, ou;* Long *i* as *igh, ie;* Base Words and Endings *–ed, –ing* (Drop Final *e*)